THE

TRANSFIGURATION OF CHRISTIANS.

A SERMON,

PREACHED AT ST. MARY'S CHURCH, OXFORD,

ON

EASTER MONDAY, APRIL 5, 1847.

BY GEORGE MOBERLY, D.C.L.,

HEAD MASTER OF WINCHESTER COLLEGE,
LATE FELLOW OF BALLIOL COLLEGE, OXFORD.

OXFORD:
JOHN HENRY PARKER.
LONDON: RIVINGTONS.   WINCHESTER: NUTT.

MDCCCXLVII.

ADVERTISEMENT.

———

It was not the intention of the author to publish this Sermon. But the representations of others, better qualified than himself to judge of the probability of its being useful in Oxford, have appeared to him to render it improper to decline to do so. He will only add that the paternal interest which he is bound to feel in a large number of young men in that beloved University makes him well pleased to offer to them even so slight a word of Christian encouragement and counsel in their progress ἀπὸ δόξης εἰς δόξαν.

Winchester College,
April 22, 1847.

A SERMON.

2 CORINTHIANS iii. 18.

But we all, with open face beholding as in a glass the glory of the Lord, are changed into the same image from glory to glory, even as by the Spirit of the Lord.

THE passage of the second Epistle to the Corinthians which, beginning at the seventh verse of the third chapter, goes on to the seventh verse of the fourth chapter, contains some of the most remarkable statements and expressions which are to be found in the New Testament of the greatness and dignity of the Christian condition. The verse which I have taken for the text (which stands at the end of the third chapter) sums up in a short space many of these statements.

The Apostle in the earlier verses of this passage has been contrasting the preaching of the Gospel, with which he himself was intrusted, with that of the Law.

Moses, he says, was commissioned by God to communicate to the people a partial dispensation of the Divine will and truth. This approach to God, and the commission which he received, did make his face to shine[a]. God's truth and revelation carried with them, as it were, a necessarily accompanying glory, so that the preacher's face be-

[a] Exod. xxxiv. 30.

came bright, and shone, and the people were afraid to come nigh him. Unveiled when he communicated with God, and talked with Him, whence the skin of his face became bright and shining, he veiled himself when he spake to the people, for they were afraid.

And yet, though thus glorious, this revelation of God's truth and will had three points of imperfection in it, or, at least, of inferiority, in comparison of the revelation with which the Apostle was intrusted.

1st, it was of the letter and not of the spirit: that is, it was throughout typical, subordinate, and unreal. It gave a visible, outward, carnal manifestation of a deeper, inward, spiritual reality which was hitherto unseen.

2ndly, it was of condemnation: for by the law is the knowledge of sin. By the law sin is made exceeding sinful[b]. The law is the strength of sin, and the wages of sin is death.

3rdly, it was temporary. Its whole force was preparatory of something further: it served as a schoolmaster to bring men unto Christ. It was instituted only in order to be done away, when the destined day should come, for the spiritual realities to take the place of the typical ritual and polity, and for the dispensation of condemnation and wrath to give way to the dispensation of mercy and forgiveness.

Glorious, however, it was nevertheless; glorious,

---

[b] Rom. iii. 20; vii. 13; vi. 23; 1 Cor. xv. 56.

because in its measure and degree a revelation from
God[c]; so glorious, that the Prophet's face shone by
whose hand it was ministered, and that the people,
who had feared to hear the voice of God speaking
to themselves lest they should die[d], could not look
even upon Moses for the brightness of his skin.
And so he veiled his face; and, no doubt, to their
great loss. Perhaps the mere necessity of his veil-
ing himself at all shewed that their hearts were too
hard to receive, even by reflection, the bright shining of the face of God; certainly the effect of it
was, that they saw not to the end of that which
should be done away. They saw in it only the
letter, only condemnation. They could see no
spirit, nor forgiveness. They could not see deep.
The veil was between them and God, and His revelation, holy, just, and good[e] as it was in itself,
uttered no other sound in their ears than literal
laws, and death on those who broke them.

And the veil which Moses wore when he spoke
to the people, is on their hearts still when they read
his written words. They see no deeper than the
letter still. They still find no pardon. Till they
turn to the Lord, who is the Spirit, the veil re-
maineth. In Him alone, and in turning to Him, is
to be found the reality which shall nullify the letter,
the forgiveness which shall overrule the condemnation, and the eternity which shall take the place of
that which is temporary.

This is their condition. "But we all," continues

the Apostle, using the state of the Jews, in order
by contrast to put forward in greater force, and
with more variety of aspect, the high state of blessing enjoyed by Christians, " we *all*"—and let it
be observed that he uses the word '*all*' though
speaking to the luxurious, quarrelsome, imperfect,
though now repentant Church of *Corinth*—we ALL,
with open, or unveiled face, behold as in a glass,
(rather, mirror as glasses,) the glory of the Lord:—
that is, our opposite, or contrasted condition. Every
Christian of Corinth, made a member of Christ, the
child of God, and an inheritor of the kingdom of
Heaven, is forthwith in the very opposite condition
to the Jews, and in a much loftier one than even
their lawgiver. The brightness of the law which
shone on Moses' face was no brightness at all in
comparison of the glory of the Lord, which shone
upon every baptized Corinthian. Between them
and the glorious revealed Lord, revealed ten times
more gloriously than even to Moses, there was no
veil. The brightness which had shone on the *face*
of Moses, now shone, with all this greater glory,
on the *hearts* of the baptized Corinthians. From
the blessed font of baptism, when the gift of the
Spirit was first given, the glory did begin to shine
upon their hearts like the sun; and every baptized man, woman, and child among them, shone
from the font with the Divine glory. " For," says
St. Chrysostom[f], " the moment we are baptized,

---

[f] Τί δέ ἐστι, τὴν δόξαν κυρίου κατοπτριζόμενοι, τὴν αὐτὴν εἰκόνα μεταμορφούμεθα;———῾Ομοῦ τε γὰρ βαπτιζόμεθα, καὶ ὑπὲρ τὸν ἥλιον ἡ

our soul shines above the sun, being purified by the Spirit, and we not only look upon the glory of God, but also thence receive a brightness on ourselves." "So much liberty and nobility we enjoy," says Theophylact, "that all of us who believe, with unveiled face (for there is no veil to the believing) mirroring the Lord's glory, are transformed into the same image, that is, we share the same glory, being as it were a mirror, and receiving His brightness, and reflecting it back. And as silver placed opposite the sun, returns some rays on being struck by the sun, so we too, who are purified in baptism by the Spirit, and shone upon by His rays, return a mental ray ourselves, and are transformed into the same image[g]."

ψυχὴ λάμπει, τῷ πνεύματι καθαιρομένη· καὶ οὐ μόνον ὁρῶμεν εἰς τὴν δόξαν τοῦ Θεοῦ, ἀλλὰ καὶ ἐκεῖθεν δεχόμεθά τινα αἴγλην. ὥσπερ ἂν εἰ ἄργυρος καθαρὸς πρὸς τὰς ἀκτῖνας κείμενος, καὶ αὐτὸς ἀκτῖνας ἐκπέμψειεν, οὐκ ἀπὸ τῆς οἰκείας φύσεως μόνον, ἀλλὰ καὶ ἀπὸ τῆς λαμπηδόνος τῆς ἡλιακῆς· οὕτω καὶ ἡ ψυχὴ καθαιρομένη, καὶ ἀργύρου λαμπροτέρα γιγνομένη, δέχεται ἀκτῖνα ἀπὸ τῆς δόξης τοῦ πνεύματος, καὶ ταύτην ἀντιπέμπει. διὸ καί φησι, κατοπτριζόμενοι, τὴν αὐτὴν εἰκόνα μεταμορφούμεθα ἀπὸ δόξης, τῆς τοῦ πνεύματος, εἰς δόξαν τὴν ἡμετέραν, τὴν ἐγγιγνομένην, καὶ τοιαύτην οἵαν εἰκὸς ἀπὸ κυρίου πνεύματος.—S. Chrysost. in loco, vol. x. p. 486.

[g] Τοσοῦτον ἀπολαύομεν ἐλευθερίας καὶ εὐγενείας, ὥστε πάντες ἡμεῖς οἱ πιστοὶ—ἀνακεκαλυμμένῳ προσώπῳ (οὐ γάρ ἐστι παρὰ τοῖς πιστεύσασι κάλυμμα) τὴν δόξαν τοῦ Κυρίου κατοπτριζόμενοι τὴν αὐτὴν εἰκόνα μεταμορφούμεθα, τουτέστι τὴν αὐτὴν δόξαν μεταλαμβάνομεν, οἷον κάτοπτρον ὄντες, καὶ δεχόμενοι τὴν λαμπρότητα, καὶ αὖθις ἀποστίλβοντες. καὶ ὥσπερ ἄργυρος ἄντικρυ ἡλίου κείμενος, ἀντιπέμπει τινας ἀκτῖνας καὶ αὐτὸς τῇ προσβολῇ τοῦ ἡλίου, οὕτω καὶ ἡμεῖς ἐν τῷ βαπτίσματι καθαιρόμενοι διὰ τοῦ πνεύματος, καὶ ταῖς ἐκείνου ἀκτῖσι καταυγαζόμενοι, αἴγλην τινα νοητὴν καὶ αὐτοὶ ἀντιπέμπομεν, καὶ μεταμορφούμεθα τὴν αὐτὴν εἰκόνα,

This then, as contrasted with the condition of the veiled heart of the Jews and their veiled prophet, is the condition of baptized Christians. The Lord, in the greater glory of the Spirit, the pardon, and the eternity, shines from the font on their unveiled hearts, giving them a glory, like the glory of the silver on which the sunbeams fall.

It is important then to observe, in the first place, that the condition of baptized Christians is spoken of here by St. Paul as a condition of *glory*. That expression, indeed, is to be found in various other passages as well as in the text. So in the seventeenth of St. John, our Lord not only speaks of being Himself glorified in His disciples, " I am glorified in them ;" but also says expressly, " the glory which thou gavest me, I have given them : that they may be one, even as we are one." Which words it will be observed, not only speak of a glory given to the Church, even as the Father gave it to the Son, but also declare that, possessing this glory, the Church should have its peculiar Divine oneness :

ἀπὸ δόξης τῆς τοῦ πνεύματος, εἰς δόξαν τὴν ἡμετέραν, καὶ τοιαύτην, οἵαν εἰκὸς ἔχειν τὸν ὑπὸ τοῦ πνεύματος τοῦ Κυρίου καὶ μηδενὶ ὑποκειμένου καταυγαζόμενον. Κύριος γὰρ ὢν, δεσποτικὰς ἔχει καὶ τὰς λαμπηδόνας. Πάντες γὰρ οἱ πιστοὶ πνεύματος ἁγίου πληροῦνται διὰ τοῦ βαπτίσματος, καὶ λάμπει αὐτῶν ἡ ψυχή· ἐπεὶ καὶ ὁ Μωσῆς ἰδὼν τὴν θείαν δόξαν, μετεμορφώθη καὶ αὐτὸς πρὸς ταύτην, τουτέστι, μετέλαβε καὶ αὐτὸς, καὶ ἔλαμπε τὸ πρόσωπον, τύπος ὢν ἡμῶν.—Theophylact in loco.

Ὡς γὰρ τὰ τοῖς ἀνθηροῖς χρώμασι παρακείμενα, ἐκ τῆς περιρρεούσης αὐγῆς καὶ αὐτὰ καταχρώννυται· οὕτως ὁ ἐναργῶς ἐνατενίσας τῷ πνεύματι, ἐκ τῆς ἐκείνου δόξης μεταμορφοῦταί πως πρὸς τὸ φανότερον, οἷόν τινι φωτὶ, τῇ ἐκ τοῦ πνεύματος ἀληθείᾳ τὴν καρδίαν καταλαμπόμενος.— S. Basil. de Sp. S. xxi.

so that as we know that that Divine oneness results from the gift of the Holy Spirit, and is designed to be the characteristic of the militant, as well as of the triumphant Church, it follows that the glory also, the glory 'as of the only-begotten of the Father,' belongs also in its degree to the Church on earth,—to the Church in its days of waiting, of warfare, and trial.

Moreover, as soon as we have thus ascertained from one place of Holy Scripture, that " glory " in some true sense of the word is the Divine property of the Church militant—glory, incipient indeed, and imperfect in comparison of that which shall be revealed hereafter, but still a glory wrought by the Spirit, shed from the face of God, mirrored on the separate Spirit-born souls of the baptized—as soon, I say, as a single passage of Holy Writ has opened our eyes to this truth, forthwith we find a host of other passages which, witnessing to the same truth, receive themselves light, and illustration, and new significancy from it. Such is the verse of the Epistle to the Colossians, " to whom God would make known what is the riches of the glory of this mystery among the Gentiles, which is Christ in you, the hope of glory," a verse in which two glories seem to be spoken of, the one, consisting in "Christ being in us," the other, which from Christ being in us, we hope for: the one the actual glory of the Christian state, the other the promised glory of the Christian hope. When again St. Paul urges the Thessalonians " to walk worthily of God who called them to his own kingdom and glory[h]," we see that we may reasonably understand a militant and a triumphant glory, as well as a militant and a triumphant kingdom.

So St. Peter writes "according as his divine power hath given unto us all things that pertain unto life and godliness, through the knowledge of him that hath called us to glory and virtue; whereby are given unto us exceeding great and precious promises: that by these ye might be partakers of the divine nature[i]."

There are very many other passages of the same kind[k], in many of which the word glory has often, unfortunately, been explained away in modern days by the allegation of a figure of speech[l], but which, literally taken, as they surely ought to be, refer it to the present militant condition of Christians and the Church. But none of all speaks more distinctly,

[h] 1 Thess. ii. 12.

[i] 2 Pet. i. 3.

[k] St. Luke ii. 32; St. John xvii. 21, 22; Rom. v. 2; viii. 30; (on which passage see the Comm. of S. Chrysostom and Theophylact); ix. 23; xv. 7; 1 Cor. ii. 7; 2 Cor. iii. 7—18; iv. 4, (τὸν φωτισμὸν τοῦ εὐαγγελίου τῆς δόξης τοῦ Χριστοῦ) 6; (πρὸς φωτισμὸν τῆς γνώσεως τῆς δόξης τοῦ Θεοῦ ἐν προσώπῳ Ἰησοῦ Χριστοῦ); viii. 23; Eph. i. 6, 12, 14, 17, 18, (ὁ πλοῦτος τῆς δόξης τῆς κληρονομίας αὐτοῦ ἐν τοῖς ἁγίοις); iii. 16; Phil. iv. 19; Col. i. 11, 27; 1 Thess. ii. 12; 2 Thess. ii. 14; 1 Tim. i. 11; Heb. ii. 10; iii. 3, 6, 14, (πλείονος γὰρ δόξης οὗτος παρὰ Μωσῆν ἠξίωται, καὶ Μωσῆς μὲν πιστὸς ἐν ὅλῳ τῷ οἴκῳ αὐτοῦ, ὡς θεράπων—Χριστὸς δὲ, ὡς υἱὸς ἐπὶ τὸν οἶκον αὐτοῦ, οὗ οἶκός ἐσμεν ἡμεῖς—μέτοχοι γὰρ γεγόναμεν τοῦ Χριστοῦ.) St. James ii. 1; 1 Pet. i. 10, 11; iv. 14, (τὸ τῆς δόξης, καὶ τὸ τοῦ Θεοῦ πνεῦμα ἐφ᾽ ὑμᾶς ἀναπαύεται); v. 10; 2 Pet. i. 3.

[l] ἐν διὰ δυοῖν.

or at such length, as the passage of the second Epistle to the Corinthians from which the text is taken. The whole structure of it acknowledges a glory in the baptized children of the militant Church—a glory greater than that which shone on the face of Moses—that glory which belongs to those who, as mirrors, reflect with unveiled face the glory of the Lord.

We all, then, beholding as in a glass the glory of the Lord—that, as we have said, is our condition—are changed—rather are changing, μεταμορφούμεθα—are *transfiguring*, into the same image. That is our course, or progress. It is at least remarkable that the Greek word here used should occur but twice in the New Testament; here, and in the narrative of the Transfiguration of our Lord. And perhaps it is to be regretted that it is not translated here by the word *transfigured*, in order thereby to carry the reader's mind at once to the natural parallel between the two passages. Natural, I say, not simply on the ground of the use of the same word in those two only places of Holy Writ, but also because the shining of the face of Moses as recorded in the book of Exodus appears to be clearly connected in the way of type or prophecy with the brighter shining of the Prophet like unto himself, which he, with Elias, witnessed on Mount Tabor.

We then are represented as undergoing a transfiguration, *from glory to glory;* from the glory of baptism to the consummated glory of salvation, ' from the glory of faith,' as St. Augustine expresses it[m], 'to the glory of sight;' from the dim, invisible glory of regeneration, to the inexpressible weight of glory of the resurrection.

Even as by the Spirit of the Lord. The change, the transfiguration which belongs to the Christian progress, is wrought by the Spirit of the Lord, and it is as by the Spirit of the Lord[n]; that is, it is in accordance with His workings, it is a true, genuine act of His almighty power of assimilation[o], whereby

[m] V. p. 1. Et propter hoc addidit *de gloriá in gloriam :* de gloriâ creationis in gloriam justificationis. Quamvis possit hoc et aliis modis intelligi quod dictum est *de gloriá in glor am :* de gloriâ fidei in gloriam speciei : de gloriâ quâ Filii Dei sumus, in gloriam quâ similes ei erimus, quoniam videbimus eum sicuti est. Quod vero adjunxit *tanquam à Domini Spiritu :* ostendit gratiâ Dei nobis conferri tam optabilis transformationis bonum.— S. Augustin., De Trinitate, lib. xv. viii. 976.

[n] Erasmus compares St. John i. 14, δόξαν ὡς μονογένους. (of which St. Chrysostom says, ὡς ἔστι βεβαιώσεως καὶ ἀναμφισβητήτου διορισμοῦ.) οἵαν εἰκὸς ἀπὸ κυρίου πνεύματος.—S. Chrysost. in loco. Cf. Philipp. ii. 12 ; St. Matt. vii. 29 ; Acts xvii. 22 ; Phil. 9, &c.

[o] There is a passage of St. Cyril of Alex. (vol. vii. p. 71.) adv. Nestorium, lib. iii., commenting on this verse :

ποία δὴ οὖν ἐν ἐκείνοις ἐξητεῖτο μόρφωσις ἡ πρός γε Χριστόν; he asks : ἢ τίνα τρόπον ἡμεῖς ἀπὸ δόξης εἰς δόξαν μεταμορφούμεθα ; ποίαν ἀφέντες μορφὴν, εἰς τίνα μεταστοιχειούμεθα ; he answers by alleging the passage of Rom. viii. 30. Ἀλλ' οἶμαι (he continues) ταυτὶ πρέποι ἂν τῇ θείᾳ τε καὶ ἀκηράτῳ διακεκτῆσθαι φύσει. κρεῖττον γάρ ἐστι καὶ ἁμαρτίας καὶ φθορᾶς, ἁγιασμὸς καὶ δικαιοσύνη· ἀναφέρει δὲ καὶ ἡμᾶς ἐν τούτοις ὁ ἐκ Θεοῦ πατρὸς λόγος τῆς θείας ἑαυτοῦ φύσεως κοινώνους ἀποφαίνων διὰ τοῦ πνεύματος. ἔχει τοίνυν ἀδελφοὺς ἐοικότας αὐτῷ, καὶ τῆς θείας αὐτοῦ φύσεως φοροῦντας εἰκόνα κατά γε τὸν τοῦ ἡγιᾶσθαι τρόπον. οὕτω γὰρ ἐν ἡμῖν μορφοῦται Χριστὸς, μεταστοιχοῦντος ὥσπερ ἡμᾶς τοῦ ἁγίου πνεύματος, ἐκ τῶν ἀνθρωπίνων εἰς τὰ αὐτοῦ. . . . Ἐνσημαίνεται δέ πως τοῖς τῆς θείας φύσεως αὐτοῦ γεγονόσι κοινωνοῖς, διὰ τοῦ μετασχεῖν ἁγίου πνεύματος, ἡ πρὸς αὐτὸν ἐμφέρεια νοητὴ, καὶ τὸ τῆς ἀρρήτου θεότητος κάλλος ταῖς τῶν ἁγίων ἐναστράπτει ψυχαῖς.

alone the soul of man could be reborn in baptism, whereby alone, so reborn, it can grow in grace, and approach more and more nearly to the likeness of the eternal Lord.

The doctrine then of this signal verse of St. Paul differs rather in *expression*, than in *substance* from the doctrine of other passages of the same Apostle. As in other passages we learn that Christian men are reborn in baptism by the Holy Spirit of God, that then they are to grow in grace and abound more and more in the gifts of the same Spirit, till they come more and more nearly to the likeness of the Lord, so in this place we are taught no other lesson in substance. It is the words only that differ. It is the glowing and glorious expressions which illustrate and brighten the substance. We learn from it that baptism gives not only regeneration, but thereby gives a glory: a glory from the face of God; a glory greater by far, and in many ways, than the glory of the face of Moses; that thenceforward we are to undergo by the working of the same glorious Spirit, a continual transfiguration; that as we mirrored, with a more dim and faint glory the likeness of the Lord at the font, so we are to become changed, after the manner of the bright shining of the Lord on Tabor, from the first glory to the last glory, from the glory which is ours when first Christ is formed in our hearts, to that perfect glory when we shall awake up after His likeness and be satisfied with it.

The doctrine, I say, is the same; but oh! how

precious are these glowing varieties of expression, these rich and glorious illustrations of phrase, and word, and allusion, wherewith the inspired Apostle gives utterance to the doctrines which he teaches. Not overstepping the exactest and severest measure of the truth of God, how does he dwell upon the loftiness, the nobleness, the wonder of the Christian state! How do the marvels of the Old Testament furnish him with contrasts, and the mysteries of the New with models, whereby he may exhibit in fresh aspects of glory and greatness the mighty doctrine with which his mind is full!

To him the condition of a Christian, baptized into Christ, is no matter of jejune and arid statement, of one precise and thorny phraseology, which admits not of other expression than a few dry unpractical words; still less is it a thing of mere sentiment, as though the doctrine of it were merely a sort of show, or spectacle, a matter to excite a certain frame of faith, or love, or other feeling in us, without any corresponding substance of truth in itself; still less again is it a mythical or poetical fiction, requiring to be reduced to the laws of rigid reason, and submitting to be interpreted on imaginary principles of human philosophy. No, it is a divine and most deep reality. To him, a Christian baptized into the body of Christ is in a condition of most exalted and amazing greatness; a condition the blessedness of which no words can transcend; a condition to which the whole of Scripture bears harmonious and conspiring witness, to produce which the whole course of the dealings of God with man had been directed since the fall.

And thus has all this richness of statement and expression a great power to guard round and protect from various enemies the truth of Christian doctrine. It defends it against the mere theologian, who would resolve the precious real revelation of God, and the wonderful facts which He doeth for us and in us, into formulæ of words and balanced phrases ; for it shews that to the Apostle's mind it was a great reality, a truth of many aspects, a *thing* and not a *word*, something to be, and to live upon, not to look at only, or hold as a tenet or proposition. It defends it against the sentimentalist, who would teach us that faith and feeling are all, and that there is little other substance in doctrine than such as may suffice to waken faith and feeling, nor inward reality and supernatural operation in the mysterious Sacraments of the Gospel; for it shews that to the Apostle's mind it was, again, a truth having substance, having real objective existence ; that Christian men are truly and really planted into the body of Christ, by a blessed baptism, possessors of a real and substantial condition of glorious *being*, *helps*, and *hopes*. It defends it against the subtler and more dangerous neologian : for it shews that the Apostle simply held what he thus richly and variously taught, and believed the sacramental admission to the body of Christ to have actually placed himself and all other Christians into a supernatural condition, and to have thereby made him and them, in title, opportunity, and heirship, partakers of the immortal life, glory, and bliss of their triumphant and ascended Lord.

But to us, brethren, who desire in all simplicity to receive the sacred words of Holy Writ, and by God's grace, to fashion our lives upon them, surely all this doctrine put forth in such high and glowing language by the Apostle is very terrible,—considering I mean, what we are, and how we live. It is no doubt awakening to read the *denunciations* of Holy Scripture ; to be told that " the wicked shall be turned into hell and all the people that forget God ;" but surely it is more awful still, particularly for those who have any reverence of spirit in them, or any generous sense of God's unspeakable mercy, and their own state of hearts, to read these wonderful sayings. Really they are more awful far than the denunciations.

It would, I suppose, be so in any state of Christian communities. It was so, it can hardly be doubted, even to the inspired Apostle himself when he gave utterance to such great and high words. For we can hardly suppose that men could ever feel in themselves that their consciousness of devotion and duty answered adequately to such lofty doctrines and statements.

But what must it be to us, who live in this generation? who are surrounded by such sights and scenes, as meet us at every moment in the present state of things in our land? how do our people live? I do not speak of the most notorious and

worst cases only, of the neglected and ignorant
population of our large manufacturing districts,
nor indeed of the poor at all, so much as of those
who know more and should be better. But our
money-getting population? our pleasure-loving
people; our political people; our literary people?
how are our children disciplined in all the land?
how are our boys trained? what are the habits of
our young men? we baptize our annual thousands
and ten thousands of infants, we help to put them
in the state which the Apostle calls a state of glory.
Each one of them is then in station, title, and heirship, more glorious than Moses, greater than the
Baptist, the greatest, up to his own day, that had
been born of women, for each one of them is a member of Christ. But how do they seem to live? how
conscious of their estate are they? do they live and
have their conversation in heaven, or in earth? in
the world of spirits, or in the world of sense?

Brethren, though there is indeed much to be
thankful for, though there are many and increas-
ing instances of Christian devotion and holy living
on every side of us, yet when we read these lofty
words of Holy Writ, and think of the actual condition of things in the mass of our countrymen,
the high and the low, the rich and the poor toge-
ther, it seems as if really the Holy Scriptures did
not *speak of us* :—as if they spoke of some long past
or Utopian condition of things, but *not of us* : as
though the words did not apply, as though the
cases were different, as though our world had

grown worse, as though there was an obvious incompatibility between the sayings of Holy Writ, and the state of our actual Christian society, and our own hearts ;—an incompatibility so obvious and so painful as almost to suggest a doubt whether the words of Holy Writ themselves might not be capable of a lower sense ; whether there might not be room for suggesting some figurative explanation, something or other to enable the world to go on as it does, in complacency and self-gratulation, without thereby disproving the very truth of Christian religion.

And such suggestions are made on many sides : by the worldly mass of educated people, who tell us that we over-interpret the Scriptures, that it is impossible to understand all these things literally ; who have no fears or uneasinesses, although every word, all those severe words, and all those glorious words, of Holy Scripture, condemn them alike ; by the so-called evangelical school, who, finding that the baptized, as a body, do not answer practically to the high words, and statements of the Scriptures, would confine all those high words and statements to those who can create in themselves a sufficiently intense fiduciary feeling to apprehend them as their own, and comfort themselves in such apprehension ; by the miserable school of real infidels, who by the application of a most unhappy, yet insurmountable philosophy, dilute the history and the creed of Holy Scripture into their own particular fancies, and so, by ready consequence, its precepts into their own particular morality.

But we know better. We know that the words of Holy Scripture are simply and divinely true. We know that we live under a supernatural system : that ministered by the Church, and with the holy use of water and Divine words, the Holy Spirit of God, the very and eternal Holy Ghost hath been infused into the hearts of Christians, making them not their own but Christ's, making them real branches of Him the vine, real members of Him who is a Divine and glorious Body : making them, yea, though many know it not, and many believe it not, and many knowing and believing it, yet do most miserably forget it, making them to possess a condition of glory and grace unspeakable, yet of glory and grace militant, not yet triumphant, of glory and grace that must yet be transfigured into higher degrees of glory and grace, even as by the Spirit of the Lord, if they are to attain at last to that which He hath set before them, which if they attain not, woe and sorrow must needs be their miserable portion.

And knowing and feeling all this, how shall we regard the state of lives, which seems to surround us on every hand ; how shall we regard our own state, the state to which, and through which our own hearts have grown up ; the recollections of our own unchastened youth, of thoughts disordered, and self-indulgent ways ?

Doubtless, there is much unseen growth of hearts ; doubtless, He who caused us to be carried by others' arms to His holy baptism, and put it into the hearts of others to undertake for us the sacred sponsorial engagements which accompanied our spiritual birth; who, in the midst of the changes, the trials, the difficulties, the losses and gains of our secret spiritual life, knoweth at each moment where and what we are, how far downward, or how far upward in our course; doubtless He, even in the midst of the sights and scenes at which our hearts are sad, and the bitter recollections with which our hearts are remorseful, is greater than our hearts and knoweth all things;—knoweth where the secret seed of spiritual life, overlaid and dormant it may be for years, may even now be ready to burst and germinate into a holy growth, though to our eyes all is dead, and cold, and hopeless as ever;—knoweth in what hearts there has been, and is, a secret unsuspected struggling of holier thoughts and prayers against sin and evil;—knoweth where unuttered (yes, and by the very person in whose heart they be, unappreciated) groanings of the Holy Spirit sound aloud in the ears of Him who knoweth what is the Spirit's mind, and heareth the intercessions which He maketh for the saints according to the will of God[p].

No doubt it is so; and blessed be God for the comfort which we may justly have in believing that it is so. And yet with every allowance that may rightly be made for such secret workings of Divine grace, still, brethren, how dark, how cold, how far from the reality of Christian life, how far from the

[p] Rom. vii. 27.

vivid reality of Scripture sayings is the aspect of our time, our people, and ourselves! How does the very heart of faith seem eaten out of this people by the love of money, the love of ease, the love of the world!

And oh! my brethren, it is by no new inventions, no new discoveries of truth, or devices of gaining power that we are to cope with this monstrous and terrible evil! The sacred Divine power is indeed with us still, in the perpetual and assured presence of the Lord with His Church until the end of the world. The machinery is still ours, in the Divine ordinances, which, through His Apostles, the Lord of the Church hath instituted to be the means of imparting His Holy Spirit to His people in all time. These are all still ours; and in these we possess what is more than sufficient to break down all the world's strongholds; to storm the treasure-house of mammon, the Babel tower of philosophy, and the dark caves of ignorance and sin. Only we must apply them faithfully : only we must not be afraid of them. They will do their work, but we must trust them; we must use them as believing in them.

Our CHILDREN must be taught, not stintingly and timidly, but clearly and boldly, how precious and invaluable a blessing they have received in being BAPTIZED into the very mystical Body of Christ our Lord. The eye of parental love, symbol and emblem of the fatherly eye of the most high God, must be on them, blessing their efforts of obedience and duty, and warning them, lest in their childish years they dim, by early disobedience, or deceit, or other sin, the pure shining of the baptismal glory.

Our BOYS must be taught that all their boyish life should be preparation for CONFIRMATION: for confirmation which should be the very strength of boyhood: confirmation, prepared for, not by a few weeks or months of partial care, but by being made the very object and end of all the instruction and training of the first youthful age. And with confirmation, for the FIRST COMMUNION: that First Communion which might be so solemn, so tender, so touching a time to a young boy's mind, which might be the very secret of sanctifying many a young heart for the trials of early life, and early death, but which is with us, alas! comparatively so little heeded!

Our YOUNG MEN must be taught, that confirmed, and become COMMUNICANTS, they have arrived at the age in which St. John calls on them for spiritual STRENGTH AND CONQUEST. "I write unto you young men, because ye have overcome the wicked one." "I have written unto you young men, because ye are strong, and the word of God abideth in you, and ye have overcome the wicked one." Christ calleth them to His bravest, most self-conquering, most angelic services. He calleth them to do battle, and to vanquish. The struggles for which the unconfirmed are yet too weak and immature; which for the elders should be passed, so that they may bring forth the quiet fruits of ascertained victory, are their very element. They are (they should be) the young and noble soldiers of the army of God: not self-indulgent, not idle, not luxurious, God forbid: not wasting on folly and frivolity the time and money which belong to nobler objects; not pardoned and half encouraged in their laxity of life by a feeble rule of law, and feebler rule of conscience which are content to hope that they will grow wiser as they grow older, and become 'respectable' before they enter into their real professional lives: but girded up to do battle against temptations from without, and temptations from within; studious, and dutiful; full of prayers; high-minded resisters of evil; pure of thought and imagination; nobly ignorant of sin; coming for continual strength to maintain their angelic battle against the evil one, to continual Communions.

And we, brethren, who are older, who have passed through our own youthful trials, whose minds are full of our own recollections, who know each one of us his own plague of heart, and separate bitterness, what must *we* do? what but *repent*? What, but offer our sad confessions before the throne of grace, and strive with all our hearts and souls that at least those who come after us may be helped and encouraged in every way to pay to God in all their lives a holier service. No one knows what is in all our hearts; no one, but ourselves and God. And what is there, is no doubt very different in each ; very different in kind, as in degree. But if we mourn over days mis-spent, and youthful sins : if we recal times when the tone of academical society and conversation did not discourage lax, self-indulgent, and even vicious living, so that our youth was not, to say the least of it, that noble, conquering youth of strength which the Apostle speaks of ;—if this be so at all with us, and to the extent that it is so, then let us turn ourselves, as to a noble and generous penance, to help in every way of encouragement and aid and example *the sanctification of our successors :* by giving them helps to prayer, *by giving them more frequent communions,* by helping them in their sacred preparations, by shewing them in our example as well as our precept, that we and they alike are admitted to a glorious condition, and are living now in trial beneath the grace of the Holy Spirit of God, desiring a perpetual transfiguration to greater degrees of glory, and looking forward to a daily nearing Judgment.

We must be *real*, and we must be *at peace*. The cause of holiness, which is the cause of God and of eternity, is too sacred and too important to be perilled for the sake of ease, or jealousy.

We must be deeply real, and we must be at Christian peace : and never was there a generation to whose hands it appeared to be more plainly entrusted to rouse a sleeping land and a slumbering Church to Christian wakefulness and vigour, and never was there a time which seemed to exhibit more awful need or to offer greater encouragement for turning the whole of our more highly educated youth, as with one accord, and in one body, into deeper and truer habits of Christian holiness and devotion.

www.ingramcontent.com/pod-product-compliance
Lightning Source LLC
Chambersburg PA
CBHW081453070426
42452CB00042B/2717

* 9 7 8 1 5 3 5 8 1 4 8 7 4 *